SMILE OF THE FACE

Compiled by
Zeenat

Published By
Creativity United

TITLE : SMILE OF THE FACE

Compiler's name : Zeenat

Published by : Creativity United

HN : 52, Main road, Kayasthagram,
Karimganj – 788719

Email: unitedwecreateabetterworld@gmail.com

ISBN: 978-93-92073-00-7

POETRY 1st Edition

PREFACE

The presented book "SMILE OF THE FACE" is a shared literary collection. Me Zeenat, the compiler, greet you all readers with all the warmth.

"Smile Of The Face" is an anthology about the smiles in people's life. There is a face in everyone's life whose smile affects them immensely. It gives us strength to live life in every moment. A smile has a great impact on us and even a forced smile has a very positive influence on our lives. So, this book reflects the ideas of the writers about "What a smile is" to each of them and about that one face, whose smile is an energy drink or a refill for their lives each day.

Hope"Smile Of The Face" will be enjoyable and resourceful for the readers...

Thank you

Zeenat

(Compiler)

COMPILER'S INTRODUCTION

ZEENAT

The author Zeenat is a school student of class 12th. She is resident of Delhi. She is interested in travelling and learning about different human behaviours. She loves to write and wants to be a world wide writer.

"Life is not about what you believe

Life is that what you live"

The Smile

There is always someone in everyone's life

Whose smile is brighter than shine

A   smile that gives a hope

A smile just simple without any scope

The magical curve on the face

That can change one's fate

The worst day can be the best

With that smile which makes the heart beats in the chest

It has the magic that can wipe tears

Give courage and can remove all of the fears

When the tired soul needs some stamina again

The smile is enough to get back the energy that drained

Zeenat

Smile Of The Face

The happy you that has lost somewhere

Gets support to again come over

Overthinking that was killing you every time

Now giving you a lot of dopamines just because of that
one smile

The calmness present in that smile

Refills you with the positivity of new life

Your soul gets a refreshment

Your eyes get the soothing

Just a smile changes you

Isn't it Amazing??

Smile – A healer

A lamp in the whole dark sky

Giving a bit of light

That's how a person smiles

To light up your dark night

Like a small wave in the quiet sea

Bringing some food from a corner of it

That smile forces itself

Just to make their loved ones live.

That One piece of straw

Falling down from the tree

That's how a smile sheds its feelings

To make your home of living

Just 2 minutes of rain

Giving slight coolness on the hot day

Smile Of The Face

Like those clouds, the smile loses itself

And try to give us relief again

And

There is a SMILE

Suffering from a thousand of pain

But hide all of the problems

To make everyone else, smile again.

And this smile can be of anyone in our life who heal our
pains even when they are in pain too!!

INDEX

Aarya Soni

The author Aarya Soni is a resident of Sohagpur, Hoshangabad. She is a medical student and persuing physiotherapy. Her hobbies are writing and singing.

तेरी मुस्कान पे वारी जाऊं..

तू कितना खूबसूरत है,तेरी मुस्कान पे वारी जाऊं..

तुझे देख देख कर मैं, यू मन ही मन मुस्काऊ,

तेरी एक मुस्कुराहट पे,मैं अपने सारे गम भुलाऊ,

तू कितना खूबसूरत है,तेरी मुस्कान पे वारी जाऊं...

तेरे इस खुशनुमा चेहरे पे,मैं अपने सारे तीरथ कराऊं,

अपने दिन रात भुला के,तुझको ही देखती जाऊं,

के तेरी मुस्कान को देख देख, मैं सतरंगी हो जाऊं,

तू कितना खूबसूरत है, तेरी मुस्कान पे वारी जाऊं

© Aarya Soni

Abhishek Bordia

The author Abhishek Bordia 27, comes from heritage city 'Ahmedabad' of Gujarat. He has worked on multiple anthologies, national magazines, and national competition. He is working on bringing on his own publication house. He is chartered Accountant and currently working in RSM India, 6th Largest Global Consulting firm as Ahmedabad practice lead. He enjoys working for national cause towards women empowerment, free medical treatment and jobs to needy. He has tied up with Unschool academy for providing courses to students at very nominal cost and assured Internships. He has further collaborated with i-Hub Gujarat ahnd eChai, startup bond venture capital management company.

Gesture of life

Spreading the smile is worthy more..

Voice echoes at the empty shore..

Cruel are wild animal... why human more?

Breads equally!! ..hope let's needy tore.

Pure water of heavenly rivers flows

Thirsty reaches them and pour the claws

Dawn in dense forests keeps us thrive

Reaching destination amongst we tries

Sensible those handicaps need help

We locate ourselves always in the map

Driver of life journeys with twisty turns

Keeping hold in whole, the most u earn.

© Abhishek Bordia

Daydreams if silly are real

Daydreams if silly!! are real
Thoughts... If laughed are truly generous!

Right ones may be tanned like shades...
Benevolent efforts put paths to mountains.

Ideology won't change. your endeavour louds..
Braggers stays whether you do better or bad in crowd.

Mistakes make people gazing at you.. if are often..
Necessary those for invincible streak u gonna form..

Letting go things is happie habit! You make.
It creates space for new ones to add on their bags...

Silent pals surrounding you observes the most...
Won't tell u much.. coz you yourself can inculcate those.

Sometimes driven by the situations!! you..
Driver!! the most trusted one and is always wid you..

Smile Of The Face

Rushing fast not gonna complete them...

Pebbles of paves anyway clutches damn..

Wen u begin it always feel long

Journey never ends until started in right tone..

A gas is necessary to hit the flame...

Fame won't felt unless you drain...

© Abhishek Bordia

Abhishek Jugran

The author Abhishek Jugran is a resident of Pauri Garhwal. He is doing BSC. His hobbies are play cricket, make cartoon paintings, reading, and singing.

My Bestie

I may smile on face,

But, you whether it is from my heart,

You have helped me through,

Right from the start,

Glad that I am in your life,

Glad that you are my friend,

With you I share my emotions so true,

There is nothing to pretend

You are and will always remain my best friend.

© Abhishek Jugran

My Mother

You are the strongest Person

I have even known.

I admire you for your Strength,

Kindness and Compassion.

You are my mother-teacher

And my best friend

I know I don't say it often enough mom,

You mean the world to me

And every year that passes

I love you even more and

I am grateful for you everyday

© Abhishek Jugran

Angela Merlin C

The author Angela Merlin C is a resident of Ramanathapuram, Coimbatore. She is a teacher of English. She is interested in penning down poems and stories.

The Beautiful Armour

Smile is the beautiful curve,

Which sets everything Straight.

She is clothed with Compassion and love

making others to forget their pain.

She is a Miracle,

Who can change the sorrows into Joy.

She is contagious,

But still the cutest and the prettiest.

She is like a sword,

Sharper and powerful.

She is the best medicine,

who can solace the dejected.

Zeenat

Smile Of The Face

So, Darling! Never Forget to smile

You've got the prettiest smile

Love! Say Cheese and move on

You have got way more to go

© Angela Merlin C

Ankita Mishra

The author Ankita Mishra is a resident of Khordha, Odisha. She is a Neet Aspirant, experience a fondness for ink for more than 3 years. Amidst the cause, the world faced during the lockdown in 2019, she discovered herself being happy in the writing field. Passing time, motivated her a lot and accelerated her pace on many platforms. She started to pen down her thoughts, worked as a co-author in many anthologies, and participated in many contests. Looking forward to becoming an Author now.

Smile For The Memory

The smile smiles at the memory,

Heading forward still miss the glimpse of the past,

How's the smile so dear to the loved ones,

Very far but found at the images of tears,

Smiles look magnificent to the realm of dreams,

Helping to move through the struggle of screams,

This is the smile that supports completing the miles,

Be a little away with patience everything gonna fine in a
while,

Here the smile with you,

Looking and staring at you,

Waiting to grab under the arms,

Here the smile devouring your charms.

© Ankita Mishra

Innocent Smile Of A Little Baby

It was raining,

Clouds were roaring,

Coldness in the air poking,

It was a night when I heard a baby crying.

Wrapped in a white cloth, small hands were wibbling,

Reducing distance when I approached him,

Finding me near, happy he seems.

Lost in his smile,

I find myself close to him,

Taking him in my arms,

My heart skips a beat seeing his adorable charms

So pure and innocent smile,

Zeenat

Smile Of The Face

My heart pumped up with its breathtaking sight,

So soft and fragile like a feather he is,

I wish he never loses his innocent smile.

© Ankita Mishra

Anshika Rajput

The author Anshika Rajput is a resident of Bulandashahar. She is a student. Her hobbies are reading books.

Smile of my face

Aaj mein baat krungi apni smile ki jo us ek insaan ko dekh ne se

aati hai, jiske liye mai sayad jada matter bhi nahi krti.

Haan, vo mujhse roj nahi milta, or nah hi jada baat krta hai,

Pr kasam se uska ek pyaara sa message bhi mujhe dheer saari

khusi de jata hai.

Jaanti hu vo apni life ko lekr bahot presan rhta hai, nahi milta

use time mujhse baat krne ka,

Pr mujhe fir bhi uske baat krne ka intezar rhta hai.

Uska vo mujhe chavvani bulana, or fir meri kisi nadaani pr

mujhe dhakkan keh dena, maano alag si khusi de jata hai.

Haan, vo baat alag hai mei usse ladti hu, irritate krti hun,

Pr dil se sirf uski khussiyo ki hi duaaen mangti hun.

Uski smile dekh kr lagta hai ki is duniya ki saari khushi ek taraf or

uski vo pyaari si mushkaan ek taraf..

Jispe mai apna sb lutaa skti hun

Haan, vo ek insaan mere jeene ki vajah hai, meri har khusi hai,

mera sara sansaar hai

Zeenat

Smile Of The Face

uska sb past present future jante hue bhi mei sapne mei bhi usse alag hona nahi chahti,

Uski ek smile ke liye meri saari khusiya kurbaan hain..!!

Uski smile hi hai, mere face ki smile ka raaj !

Yes, I proudly say the reason of my smile is my Aathanni!!

© Anshika Rajput

Anveshitha

The author Anveshitha is a resident of Hyderabad, Telangana. She is a Home maker. She is interested in cooking and writing.

It was a smile of

It was a smile of hate,

It was a smile of pain,

It was a smile of sadness,

It was a smile of anger.

It was a smile of mock,

It was a smile of sarcasm,

It was a smile of sinister,

It was a smile of evil.

It was a smile of ego,

It was a smile of jealousy,

It was a smile of possessiveness,

It was a smile of attitude.

It was a smile of pride,

It was a smile of respect,

It was a smile of dignity,

It was a smile of thoughts.

Zeenat

Smile Of The Face

It was a smile of success,

It was a smile of failure,

It was a smile of profit,

It was a smile of loss.

It was a smile of happiness,

It was a smile of loneliness,

It was a smile of problems,

It was a smile of solutions.

It was a smile from heart,

It was a smile from soul,

It was a smile of our emotions,

It was a smile of our thoughts.

The smile on one's face is a replica of their emotions and

heart.priy

© Anveshitha

Aritraja Mukherjee

The author Aritraja Mukherjee is a resident of north 24 Parganas, Kolkata. She is persuing bachelor's degree in English. She is interested in writing and painting.

Smile

Smile!

For you have a million hearts to win.

Smile!

Because you are distinct.

The roads are bad

But the wind kisses good;

Your aim is reached

When it sounds like a parody to me.

I am the world where you fight.

The barrier I build

Is hard to leap,

But you succeed!

Now Smile again!

To walk upon this lonely path;

Now Smile more!

Isn't the goal reached?

© Aritraja Mukherjee

Aayushi Singh

The author Aayushi Singh is a resident of Manendragarh, Koriya. She is Content Writer. She is interested in writing, drawing and reading.

खुशी

किसी की मुशकुराहत बन सखो तो

उसे कहते हैं खुशी

किसी के गम को बात सखो तो

उसे कहते हैं खुशी

जिंदगी सिर्फ जीने का नाम नहीं है जनाब

किसी को जिंदगी जीना सिखा सखो तो

उसे कहते है खुशी

किसी को बिन वजह हसा सखो तो

उसे कहते हैं खुशी

खामोसियों में दबे गम को मिटा सखो तो

उससे कहते हैं खुशी

सुकून के पल जीने को हम भटकते हैं जो

किसी के गम मीठा कर सुकून पा सखो तो

उसे कहते हैं खुशी

© Aayushi Singh

खुशियो के रंग

आज खिलते हुए रंगो से कुछ सिखते हैं में

चलो आज इन रंगो की तरह खिलते हैं

हर किसी की जिंदगी में गम के बादल तो होते है

चलो आज खुशियो के कुछ रंग भिखेरते है

चलो आज इन रंगो की तरह खिलते हैं

इन्द्रधनुष सी चमक लिए

इस जग को रोशन करते हैं

चलो आज बेरंग जिंदगी को रंगो से भरते हैं

काले गोरे का भेद छोर के

आज इस दिल का मेल धोते हैं

चलो आज खुबसुरत रंगो से रिश्ते पिरोते

है चलो आज खुशियो के रंग बिखेरते हैं...

© Aayushi Singh

Chandni Baid

The author Chandni Baid is a resident of Udaipur. She is a Cs. Her hobbies are Penning thoughts that are related to real world.

मेरी इश्क को तुम्हारी मोहब्बत !

चलो एक रोज मेरे इश्क़ को तुम्हारे मोहब्बत से मिलाते हैं..

फिर उनको एक दूजे से प्यार करने का सलीका समझाते है !!

जो ना हो पसंद तुम्हें वो में ना करू...

ओर जो हो पसंद मुझे वो तुम कर गुजरो !!

तरीका थोड़े से तुम अपनाओ मेरे मोहब्बत ए अंदाज़ का...

थोड़ासा सबक में सिखु तुम्हारे बयान ए अंदाज़ का!! एहसासों को

दिल की पेटी से खोलकर तुम रखदो अल्फाजों में सज़ा कर..

थोड़ा सा में अल्फाजों को संवार लूं जज्बातों की चादर ओढाकर!!

मेरी खुशियों का ख्याल रखो तुम...

तुम्हारी मुस्कान में बन जाऊं हर कदम!!

खुदसे पहले मुझे रखो हर वक़्त ओर घड़ी में...

में भी खुदको तुमको समर्पण कर बेठू हर पल ओर सदी में!!

मुझे जो और जैसा चाहिए तुम खुदको वैसा ढाल लो..

में तुम्हारे रंग में खुदको रंग दूं ऐसा हर हाल हो!!

चलो एक रोज मेरे इश्क़ को तुम्हारे मोहब्बत से मिलाते हैं...

फिर उनको एक दूजे से प्यार करने का सलीका समझाते है!!

© Chandni Baid

सुना हैं !!

सुना है ...

उसको लोग देखने को तरसते हैं

तो चलो आज उसके शहर ठहर के देखते हैं

सुना है ..

उसकी बातों से मिश्री टपकती हैं

चलिए आज उसकी बातों में खुद को घोलकर देखते हैं

सुना है ....

उसकी चंचल सी मुस्कान से दिन की शुरुआत होती हैं

चलो फिर आज एक हसीन सवेरा का आगाज़ होते देखते है

सुना है ....

उसकी आंखों के अश्क से लोगो के जीवन में गम की बारिश हो

उठती हैं चलिए आज उस बारिश में भीगकर उसके अश्कों को

पोंछकर देखते हैं

सुना है ...

उसकी दुआओं से मुर्दे में भी प्राण आजाए

चलो फिर आज फिर उसपे मर कर देखते हैं

© Chandni Baid

Deependar Singh

The author Deependar Singh is a resident of Meerut, Uttar Pradesh. He is a You tuber and writer. His hobbies are writing and singing.

तेरी एक मुस्कान

तेरी एक मुस्कान के बदले ये सारा जहांन ठुकराया मैने

मुझे तेरी आदत हो गई है सिर्फ खुदा से बताया मैंने

तुझे तो मालूम ही होगा आंखे बड़ी मासूम है मेरी

तेरी एक मुस्कान के खातिर तेरे पैरों को आंसू से नहलाया मैंने

जब तुझे एहसास हुआ मेरे होने का तेरी कोख में

चेहरे पर मुस्कान थी और आंखों को भिगोया तूने

जीने की तमन्ना ले कर तेरे जिस्म से अलग जब हुआ मैं

मुझे हंसता देख कर सारा दुख दर्द बुलाया तूने

तेरी ही मुस्कान और चाहत थी मेरी मां

जो बेखौफ जिंदगी को बिताया मैंने

जब किसी ने तेरी मुस्कुराहट का कारण पूछा

तो नाम अपने बेटे का बताया तूने

जब पूछा किसी ने तेरे जीने का कारण

तो नाम अपने दीप का बताया तूने

© Dipendar Singh

Dr Irfan Ali

The author Dr. Irfan Ali is a resident of Baghpat, Uttar Pradesh. He is a Physiotherapist. His hobbies are writing and listening music.

उसकी प्यारी मुस्कान

अब और क्या लिखु

उसकी पयारी मुस्कान के बारे मे

बस यू समझ लो जैसे

चाँद चमकता है लाखो सितारो मे

उसकी मुस्कान अंधेरे मे

उजाला सा लगती है

रोशन हो जाती है जिन्दगी हमारी

जब वो मुस्कुरा दिया करती है

उसकी मुस्कान से ही जैसे

ये दुनिया चमकती है

अब और क्या लिखु

Smile Of The Face

उसकी प्यारी मुस्कान के बारे मे

बस यू समझ लो

जैसे चाँद चमकता है लाखो सितारो मे

उसको देखा था जब पहली बार

वो सरमाते हुए मुस्कुराए थे

हम अपना दिल और जान

उसी पल उन्हे दे आये थे

उनके मुस्कुराने से ही सायद

मेरे जीवन मे बहार है

उसके होने से है बागो मे महक

उसकी मुस्कान से ही फूलो पर निखार है

अब और क्या लिखु

उसकी प्यारी मुस्कान के बारे मे

बस यू समझ लो जैसे

चाँद चमकता है लाखो सितारो मे।

© Dr. Irfan Ali

प्यार की मुस्कान

क्या लिखु उसकी मुस्कुराहट के लिए

उसकी एक मुस्कुराहट ने हमारे होश उडा दिये

हम होश मे आने ही वाले थे

कि वो फिर से मुस्कुरा दिये

उसकी मुस्कुराहट का हमपर कुछ ऐसा असर हुआ

वो मुस्कुरा दिये तो जीवन हसी

उनके आने से पूरी हुई हर कमी

वो अगर खुल कर हस दे तो खिल जाते है गुल कयी

उसकी मुसकुराहट ही है वजह

जो लगने लगी दुनिया हसी

मुसकुराहट उसकी कुछ यू कमाल है

Smile Of The Face

क्या लिखु मुस्कुराहट पर उसकी यही अब सवाल है उसकी मुस्कुराहट ने

तो हमे लबज ही भूला दिये क्या लिखु उसकी मुस्कुराहट के लिए उसकी

एक मुस्कुराहट ने हमारे होश उडा दिये मुस्कुराने का हुनर उसने परियो से

सीखा होगा मुझे तो लगता है उसकी मुस्कुराहट के आगे परियो का हुस्न भी

फीका होगा उसकी मुस्कुराहट से मेरे जीवन मे बहार है कोई जाकर बताए

उसे कि उसकी मुस्कुराहट से हमे अपने जीवन से ज्यादा प्यार है उसकी

मुस्कुराहट ने हमारे छक्के छुडा दिये क्या लिखु उसकी मुस्कुराहट के लिए

उसकी मुस्कुराहट ने हमारे होश उडा दिये

© Dr. Irfan Ali

Jagath Narayanan J

The author Jagath Narayanan. J, a second year UG student from English department at PSG COLLEGE OF ARTS AND SCIENCE-COIMBATORE.

He has published many poems in the books entitled DAWN TO DUSK, GROWING & GLOWING, FRIENDS FOR LIFE, THE SHADES OF MUSINGS and A PENNY FOR YOUR THOUGHTS.

Practicing grammar topics is his cup of tea.

The Revitalizer

Wherever in our lives, the only revitalizer is someone's smile.

To live our lives as keen as mustard with no regrets over our

past

Is to make someone feel as cool as cucumber,

When he/she in a tight corner.

Our lives are as clear as mud;

Leading us to many undisclosed paths

With several unresolved, indefinite worries

Filled in our soul, however,

We may handle our lives as fresh as Daisy

By just feeding street dogs.

Dogs can also smile, reveal its love of faith,

That is as strong as our love.

It doesn't matter whether our assistance is enough or not;

What really matters is our timely assistance will make them as

happy as Larry.

Having the habit of helping, the most expensive quality is

what we need now.

The only manner to relieve ourselves from

The worldly sorrows is to make someone feel untroubled.

Smile Of The Face

Beaming someone's heart isn't so complex as nerves of our

Brains.

The world has lost her blissful look,

Owing to human's inhumane actions

That have been performed over the past centuries.

Everyone has been longing for someone to make him/her

shine,

So don't let this long longingness as an unquenchable one.

© Jagath Narayanan J

Jatin Barewar

The author Jatin Barewar is a resident of Gondia, Maharashtra. He is an Engineering Undergraduate. His interests make him feel connected with the world and calms his heart and mind.

Smiling hope

When the rain doesn't stop

And I can't make it home,

When everything's darkness

And I feel so alone,

In desperate hope I go and search for her in all the

corners of my house;

I didn't find her(mumma) .

I hope she is happy with her life

I hope she is happy with her son

I hope she see what I have done

I hope she is safe in this world

Like a bird on the tree, I hope she is free

I sit alone and pray,

And cling to love so true,

Zeenat

Smile Of The Face

I hope to see her once today

I die loving her.

When family was pain,

When friends can't be found,

When I just want to scream

But I found her around,

When it's not my fault,

And I feel like I am done, Just wait for the her.

The sunshine will come.

The blossom will always flourish,

The seasons will always change.

People come and go,

Their shadows comforting and strange.

But she will be same

I will get stronger.

Zeenat

Smile Of The Face

Days will get longer.

Hope will flourish, Memories to cherish.

When everything seems to be dark there is always a hope

of sunshine.

© Jatin Barewar

उम्मीद की खुशी

उम्मीद,

उम्मीद कितना छोटा शब्द है न, कहते हैं कि जीवन में

उम्मीद ना हो तो समझो कुछ नहीं है।

उम्मीद है तो सब कुछ है

उम्मीद एक अहसास या हौंसले की तरह होती है।

इसका कोई रूप-रंग नहीं है, लेकिन हर आदमी इसी के सहारे

ज़िंदा है।

कितना अजीब है न।

कहते हैं कि उम्मीद अगर जीत की रखो तो जीत मिलती है,

हार की रखो तो हार मिलती है।

क्या इतनी बेशकीमती होती है उम्मीद?

Smile Of The Face

दिन भर की थकान, तनाव, चिडचिड, हताशा ईन सब के बाद

जब हम सोने जाते हैं,

एक उम्मीद ही तो है कि नया सवेरा नयी उम्मीद लेकर

आएगा।

जनाब एक उम्मीद ही तो होती है जिसके सहारे इंसान सारी

उम्र काट लेता है उम्मीद ही तो होती है जिसके सहारे एक

शाहिद की बेवा जिंदगी काट लेती है

एक उम्मीद ही तो है कि समाज अपराध, भ्रष्टाचार, द्वेष,

ईर्षा, प्रदुषण रहित होगा!

जनाब उम्मीद पर ही दुनिया कायम है

उम्मीद के बिना कुछ नि किया जा सकता,

उम्मीद वो चीज है जो व्यक्ति हारने से पहले करता है,

उम्मीद वर्षों से दहलीज पर खड़ी वो मुस्कान हैं, जो हमारे

कानो मे धीरे से कहती है,

अब सब ठीक होगा बस मुस्कराते रहिये

© Jatin Barewar

Johana Miracline S S

The author Johana Miracline S S is a resident of Coimbatore. She is pursuing master degree in English. She is interested in writing and nature.

Lovely smile

Smile grin like a Cheshire cat

It's ray is magical it beam spread

That penetrates and seep into

The spread it's tentacles

That could arise from an unco

albeit sanctioned in pleasent mode

Washes out the inner rage

Something magical that could be

Brought out easier but typically

On others, even if their doesn't wish too

Express out its swear out

The inner emotion and softling

© Johana Miracline S S

Keshab Satpathy

The author Keshab Satpathy is a resident of Bhubaneswar, Odisha. He is a student of humanities class 12th. His hobbies are writing, painting, and writing.

Munni

I remember the day she came home

Would jump around like a little storm

Like a fluffy ball she looked

Black like coal and white like milk

Patches on her body gently hooked

Slept with me like a baby on my arm

And woke up with me to the morning alarm

Taught me what a father's love felt like

She looked at me like i was her world

And may be she knew that she was mine too

One day she went out for a whole day and night

I panicked to the core with all my fright

I knew she must move around as she grew up

But what to do? I denied my kitty was a cat now.

© Keshab Satpathy

The lady with the grape

I met this old lady while we went for a charity drive. Sitting by the corner of a temple she held few grapes in her hand. I went to her, gave her food and water and turned to walk away while all of a sudden she called me back. Handed me the grapes that she held and said, "this is all i could give you in return for the love and kindness you gave me" i sat down, and ate the grapes while sharing them with her. I felt the need of kindness. Both for her and for myself. She found kindness in my actions and i found it in her reaction.

© Keshab Satpathy

KING IDR

The author King Idr is a resident of Meerut, Uttar Pradesh. He is an accountant, writer and singer. His hobbies are writing and singing.

The curvy reaction (smile)

The curvy reaction that

Make you beautiful too much

The best way to face every problem

And also to remove grudge

it love to stay below your nose and

give shape to your lips and eyes

it is helpful in removing pain and

make you compassionate to others

it adds value to your face

And keep balance all the relations

it is somewhere the sign

of opening your heart

it is better than all languages

and better than all the words

it help you whether you are employee

or you are running any business

© King Idr

Real man never cry

Real man never cry

They smile in every trouble

Because they welcome problem

Like their strength is gonna double

They appreciate everything

Whatever they have

Because they know for every trouble

Enough is the curvy bubble

They love beauty of their soul

They never get angry on small things

They respect every emotion

So they never stop smiling

They love to write the thoughts

With their happy expression

Because smiling face is never out of fashion

And they never like to falling

© King Idr

Laxmi Singh

The author Laxmi Singh is a resident of Burdhaman, West Bengal. She is pursuing BA Hons. She is interested in reading and writing.

खासियत

खासियत सागर की गहराई में नहीं,

क्षितिज के साक्षात्कार में है।

खासियत सूर्य के अलंकार में नहीं

चंद्रमा के अंधकार में है।

मोल आंसुओं का नहीं,

उसकी छिपी मुस्कान में है।

इस दुनिया के शोर से दूर,

खासियत खामोश आवाज में है।

संदिग्ध है मुझे उस मुस्कुराहट पर

जो सत्यता का पात्र नहीं,

देखा है मैंने उस मासूमियत को,

जो अब इस मुस्कान में नहीं,

कशमकश ख्वाहिशों में नहीं,

उलझन जरूरतों के दौर में।

सम्मान मौन मे नहीं,

सम्मान बुलंदी की आवाज में है।

जिंदगी की दौड़ से दूर,

आज सब कुछ भूल जाते हैं।

तमीज और आंसुओं से परे,

थोड़ा बेवजह मुस्कुराते हैं।

खासियत हकीकत में नहीं,

ख्यालों के बेपरवाह अंदाज मे है।

खासियत छिपे राज में नहीं,

उसकी हल्की-सी मुस्कान में है।

© Laxmi Singh

Manisha Baskaran

The author Manisha Baskaran is a resident of Thyagarajanagar, Tirunelveli. She is professor of Civil Engineering. She is interested in book collections and writing.

Smile after a cry

A small upward curve in our face,

Is the most energetic emotion that shows our craze.

It reflects the irrefutable valour,

When it's witnessed in the defeated soldier.

That's a sign of confidence and perseverance,

Once I smiled forgetting the pain, Now I'm smiling with it's

remembrance.

There is a tremendous difference between both,

But never let the folks, who stands with you in your fall and

growth.

© Manisha Baskaran

Song of the day

It was a breezy morning, I jogged effortlessly

There ran a song in radio, I heard the jazz closely

The tune started to embed in mind and echoed more

It posses the power of attraction as a mesmeric lure

The lyrics dashed all over the nuke of my head

The crave made me to hum the harmony to the world

At that dusky balcony, I'm slightly composed,

I overheard the music nearby, followed by a grisly noise

I stampede all over the treads of the stairs and reached the
TV

Turned the channel back and finally attained my visual
victory.

© Manisha Baskaran

Pratham Shukla

The author Pratham Shukla is a resident of Varanasi. He is a student. He is a music junkie and loves traveling.

मेरा प्यारा गांव

खेतो की मेड़ों पर घूमे धूल लगी हो पांव में,

आओ हम सब लौट चले अपने प्यारे गांव में.

जहा सुबह नित आया करती गीत सुरीले साज लिए,

बैलो की मधमस्त चाल हो खुशियों को सौगात लिए.

आपस में पंछी बतियाते सीधे सरल स्वभाव में,

आओ हम सब लौट चले अपने प्यारे गांव में.

जहा रोज दिवस घर गूंजा करते बच्चो की किलकारी से

देवी और देवता पूजे जाते भाव अभाव में

आओ हम सब लौट चलेअपने प्यारे गांव में.

जहा घरों में बाते होती सबसे प्रेम सम्मान की,

जहा घरों में पूजा होती बड़े बुजर्ग इन्सान की,

जहा बरगद और पत्थर भी पूजे जातें श्रद्धा भाव में

आओ हम सब लौट चले आपने प्यारे गांव में

© Pratham Shukla

Priyanshu Shekhar

The author Priyanshu Shekhar is a resident of Shastri Nagar, Munger. He is interested in reading, writing, listening to music and songs

My Happiness of Life

The feeling of happiness she is,

The feeling of joy she is,

The feeling of contentment she is,

The feeling of love she is,

The feeling of life she is,

Her smile is a way to live life again,

Her smile is a ball of sunshine in the cold winter,

Her smile is light in the darkness of life,

In her smile, I see something more beautiful than the stars,

In her smile, I see something brighter than the moon and

stars,

Her smile gives me a reason to live my life again,

In my darkest days, her smile is the guiding light to me,

On my worst days, her smile is what keeps me sane,

Zeenat

Smile Of The Face

In my pain, her smile is the cure and relief to me,

In my happiness, she is the joy and satisfaction to me,

In my failures, her smile is the motivation for me,

In my success, her smile is the reward for me.

True this feeling is for me,

My happiness in life she is,

My satisfaction in life she is,

My feeling of love she is,

My feeling of life she is,

My reason to live life she is.

© Priyanshu Shekhar

You are My Angel of Life

Like an angel, you smile,

Like an angel, you laugh,

Like an angel, your eyes shine,

Like an angel, your face glows,

Like an angel, you entered my life,

An angel without wings you're,

Brighter than the moon and stars you're,

My angel of life you're.

Your angelic smile is bliss to me,

Your angelic smile is peace to me,

Your angelic smile is a joy to me,

Your angelic smile is the satisfaction to me,

Your angelic smile is the ball of sunshine to me,

Your angelic smile is the Venus to me.

Zeenat

Smile Of The Face

Oh! how much I adore your smile,

Oh! how much I admire your smile,

Oh! how much I love your smile.

My Venus of Life you're,

My Angel of Love you're,

My Angel of Life you're,

My Angel you're.

© Priyanshu Shekhar

P·Puviyarasu

The author P. Puviyarasu is a resident of Thiruvannamalai. He is a Student. His interest is to enjoy his life.

Dream

A teen young chasing his dreams grown in a well settled situation and grown in a comfort zone, the gem of his family. After completing his graduation he decided to stand oh his feet and started cahsing his dreams, after many failures and hard lucks he got placed in a company and started working for it. Inspite of many struggles he continued for his goals, days went on he worked without giving up and a month got over and received his first month's salary.

Though he needed many things for him, he decided to buy gift for his lovely mom and his hero (Dad) and when he reached home and suprised them, they felt proud of him, at that moment the precious smile at their face made his day and a great memory to be remembered life long...

Anything in this world can be given to make them smile but even a small thing with your efforts and earning matters a lot

Zeenat

to them. If u feel that smile on their face because of your

efforts, then u will feel that pleasure then nothing seems to

be more valuable than that. Make your parents smile and feel

happy for you.

© P. Puviyarasu

Her smile

A teen age boy's love story.

A 18 years old boy after completing his schooling joined

college, a new place and a new beginning he made friends

and enjoyed his days.

Days went on..All these days he has came across many girls

but his eyes a turned for a girl at his class, he started to fall

for her, Her powerful eyes melted him but the most beautiful

thing is Her Smile.. which made him to smile with no reasons.

Seeing her with the smile on her face is the most prettiest

thing in the world which he felt as his happiness..

He felt that anything in the world can be done to make her

smile..

Day by day His heart started longing and every day started to

see her smile.How bad, rough and tough is day was,Her smile

gave the peace to him and the strenghth to move on.Her

smile became his strength, hope, happiness and everything.. and he started moving with her cute smile hoping for the magic to happen. And here the story of the pure love for Her smile without any expectations, Just always expecting to see Her smile for his lifetime ends here.

© P. Puviyarasu

Rangeesh Chandrasekar

The author Rangeesh Chandrasekar is a resident of Chennai. He is a MBA Finance and Marketing graduate. He is interested in writing.

Smile on the face

The easiest thing to get from a person but once lost it becames the hardest to get back. Trust affects people emotionally but in a good and a bad way. Firstly in a relationship it can't be formed without trust otherwise you struggle and that struggle leads to anxiety and you start to over think but once you trust that person you love. You're never overwhelmed with anxiety just a smile on your face whenever you think about them. And that's why trust is so highly valid in a relationship it becames the backbone of the relationship.Trust helps us grow and helps us form an emotional bond with the person you trust as we human beings are social beings and can't do everything by ourselves without help. Smile as much as you trust you.

© Rangeesh Chandrasekar

S·K·Shanmugapriya

The author S.K Shanmugapriya is a resident of Kumbakonam. She is Medical student and Pursuing pharm-D (Doctor of pharmacy). Her hobbies are writing and singing.

Mom's smile

The best feeling moments my mom's smile,

seeing that smile,

feeling that smile,

I am totally immersed with her love.

Even though me and mom are apart from each other,

I can go through the bad times just remembering with her

smile alone

Her smile always brings me,

her hug gives me hope,

her kiss gives me energy,

touch gives me boldness,

presence gives me courage,

her smile gives me cure.

© S.K Shanmugapriya

Smiley face.

1)   Dear mom,

From holding my hands to holding our soul,

Let's be together.

2)   Mom's smile is best make up in her face I ever seen.

3)   Widening both side of lips,

Eyes filled with joy,

that's her smile.

© S.K Shanmugapriya

Saswat Kumar Panda

The author Saswat Kumar Panda is a resident of Aska, Ganjam. He is a Law Student. His hobbies are reading, writing and traveling.

Way of success in life

Smile is the best thing that a human being possess. Smile is such a thing that transforms a human from sadness to happiness. A person may be very sad but whenever he or she sees any other person in a happy mood, then all his sadness fades away. There are many persons who has the in-built quality of spreading happiness. They are storehouse of happiness. They spend their entire life in spreading happiness and making other happy.

Every individual has such a person in life who recedes the sadness and insert the dose of happiness in life. In my life also, there are several individuals who are the reason for my existence in life. Every child is always fond of his/her parents and a single smile on their parents is clearly reflected in the

life of the child. The smile of my parents create a glow in my

face and it acts as a support system for the entire life. Their

smile enhances the spirit of the life that ultimately acts as the

support system of life. Another important person in my life

was my Dada (my father's eldest brother). He was my role

model and his smile was more precious than the diamond. His

smile always created a flow of self-satisfaction and increases

the hope in life and destiny. He always used to say about the

good things and doing the right things in life. He was an ideal

teacher who always taught his students about the great

philosophy of life. His greatness is still being enhanced in

every path of my life and would always continue to do further for the rest of my life. Sadly, he is not present with us

anymore as the divine God has called him soon. Although he

is not present with us anymore, still his thoughts, teachings,

motivation, inspiration are with us forever. He is still present

in my mind and heart. I can't forget him and his vision of

success in life. My siblings are also one of my reason for

happiness.

In my life, every individual is of utmost importance as each

and every individual plays a significant role in my life both

directly and indirectly. The presence of everyone in my life

creates a good and positive vibe and it always inspires to do

the right thing in life and to judge the life not according to

monetary aspects but according to spiritual and moral

aspects. Happiness is not just a thing or an expression but it is

an emotion and feeling that cheer up our heart and gives us a

path to move forward in our life. Whenever you see an

individual in joyful and cheerful mood, then automatically,

your mind becomes cool and you have a reason to be happy.

© Saswat Kumar Panda

Satyam Tiwari

The author Satyam Tiwari is a resident of Lucknow. He is a MA Student. His hobbies are watching anime, writing stories, reading.

Smile

Her smile helped me to let go off the pain

As old flower die & new petal takes birth

New life waits as drought of sadness was ended by her smiles
of rain

I walked a step, she smiled more, I saw a beautiful smile on
the earth.

Her smile is like a lotus in a pond

Many failures she has seen yet she grows every time strong

Her smile hides many taunts yet she ties her family with a
love bond.

She forgets her pain when she sees other pain, she warms
them with her smile all day long

She knows that rose will wither one day

She chose to smile till her last day.

© Satyam Tiwari

Zeenat
101

Her smile

It was raining and Shyam was riding his bike in a hurry.

The road was slippery & wet due to rain.

Shyam took a right turn,

and a young girl came in front of him.

Shyam tried his luck but he couldn't control it because of the
wet road, & speed.

Bike hit the girl, she fell down, blood came out of his
forehead.

Shyam said,"I am sorry girl"

Girl got up, "It's ok brother, how are you?"

Shyam's jaw drops, "let's go to hospital, how are you calm?"

Girl smiles, "I got hurt, but I am happy that both of us are
okay, & only strong people smile."

Shyam took her to the doctor & learned the value of a smile.

© Satyam Tiwari

Zeenat
102

Shipra Singh

The author Shipra Singh is a resident of Kanpur, Uttar Pradesh. She is a student. Her hobbies are Writing and travelling.

Twinkling faces

Twinkling faces.... Ha... Ha... It's now difficult to find

People nowadays hassling each other to become superior.

For me.. Mine own smile make my day

Because self smiling face can make Wrosely things into right way...

I think every smiling face hold magical Encense, which work as pain cure...

And help to sail out through worse phase of life stage.

Smile has great phenomenon which make atmosphere lighter and happier....

So let smile and also make others smile

It will help bleeding wounds to fill up faster....

Also expression less faces will get new life in them....

© Shipra Singh

Zeenat
104

Simplest Smile

Peace began with smile...

Friendship began with smile

Tempered faces also loose angryness beside one smile..

Smile can fill one empty space with life of wonders

This smile is sign of oneness of society.

It is very much cureable medication for traumatic person.

So.. begin every journey of life with cutest smile

Because after all one day we all have to leave this universe...

Smile is one wonder thing which God has given to human...

So... Let use it...and live life with full craziness and madness..

So that while leaving this world we should not have pockets of

regret....

© Shipra Singh

Zeenat

Sneha Chavan

The author Sneha Chavan is a resident of Mumbai, Maharashtra. She is a student. Her hobbies are writing, dancing and gardening.

ज़िंदगी

माफ़ करना जिंदगी मैंने तुझे गलत समझा,

मैंने हर बार तुझे अपने आप से अलग समझा...

मैंने हर वक्त हर कदम पर तुझे धोका दिया ज़िंदगी,

पर तुझे अपने वफादारी से मुझे चौका दिया ज़िंदगी..!

तूने इतना तड़पाया, कि लगा तु बड़ी जालिम है;

फ़िर समझ आया ये ख़ुद से लड़ने की तालीम है.

ज़िन्दगी, इक बार फुरसत से मिलना मुझे;

अब तलक के लिए शुक्रिया कहना है तुझे...

माफ़ करना जिंदगी मैंने तुझे गलत समझा,

मैंने हर बार तुझे अपने आप से अलग समझा..!

© Sneha Chavan

तराश

आज मेरे पास वक्त ही वक्त है,

सोचा थोड़ा ख़ुद को निहार लू।

बड़े दिनों बाद फुरसत से

आइने में खुद को देखा।

ऐसा लगा की वो कोई और है,

जो आइने में थी वो मै ना थी.!

आंखे, उसके नीचे के काले घेरे थे.

मानो अंधेरे में उजाले की उम्मीद में थे.

बाल जो अब सफ़ेद हो चुके है:

जैसे अंधेरी रात, तारों से भरी हो।

चेहरे पर जो नूर हुआ करता था,

अब उसकी जगह झुर्रियों ने ले ली है।

आंखो में काजल हुआ करता था,

अब उसकी जगह चश्मे ने ली है,

सारा बदन थक सा गया था:

मानो कोई हराभरा पेड़ सुख सा गया था..!

जिंदगी को जीना था क्या पता कैसे

मुझ से बस वो टकराकर निकल गई,

ताउम्र रेत की तरह हाथों से फिसल गई।

मैंने ढूंढ़ना चाहा ख़ुद को बेवजह,

आज में, कल में, अतीत में, हर जगह

मेरे कई टुकड़े मिले मुझे सब जगह,

जाने कैसे मै ख़ुद से रूठती गई:

ज़र्रा ज़र्रा करके यूं टूटती गई।

मैंने मेरे हर इक टुकड़े को समेट लिया,

जिसे जहां होना था उस वहां जोड़ दिया।

ख़ुद के बिना बड़ी अधूरी थी जिंदगी:

ख़ुद को अपना कर आज पूरी है ज़िंदगी

© Sneha Chavan

Somnath Misra

The author Somnath Misra is a resident of South 24 parganas. He is a Purohit. He is interested in art, photography, traveling, volunteering.

You're somebody's reason to smile

It is my fathers smile that give me a way to live life again as he can change any negativity into supreme positivity. His eyes give a ocean of strength to me. His smile make me able to let go ever worse moment in my life.His smile make me feel that i can achieve everything that I want to do.His way of living life inspires not only me but also to every member of our house.Goal of a life is to be successful in every aspect. My father's way of living and achieving inspires me to set higher goals. His way shows me the path.

© Somnath Misra

Zeenat

111

Dr Sudipta Mishra

The author Sudipta Mishra is a resident of Puri, Odhisa. She is Persuing PhD. She is interested in writing and dancing.

A message from Heaven

I am in my dream place

Oh, hear! This place is laced with kindness

Don't think about my wellness

Everyone welcomed me with a happy face

I sit down and sail with the floating clouds

I fly high amidst the stars and dance in a crowd

Oh, God, it's wonderful to breathe in such an eternal world

I roam freely by sucking the nectar without any bound

I crave to hold this moment forever,

Suddenly, I realise it's just a nightmare of a cracked core!!!

© Sudipta Mishra

Zeenat
113

Smile and Feel the Joy of Life

Spare a moment to relive

To release from the agonies of past

To rejoice in the glory of Earth

To feel the aura of loving hearts

Live in the present moments

Dance with the blue waves

Smile in the dusky twilight of the sky

Feel the magic of thy lover's eyes

Pause and wait for the happy days

Forge to the point of ecstasy

Bask in the yellow rays of the Sun

Bathe in the salty water of the Sea

Let your arms embrace the serene night

Zeenat

Smile Of The Face

May you freeze in such overwhelming sight

Embrace the light by omitting your fright

Learn to let go of moments that can crush your mind

Live and let live others to create a moment of delight

Breathe and stimulate your living spirit

© Sudipta Mishra

Sweetlin Anisha· R

The author Sweetlin Anisha R is a resident of Sowripalayam, Coimbatore. She is PG English Literature. She is interested in music and travelling.

Her smile

She got her wrinkles in face

White smoked eye balls

Quivering body

Still I catches her frickled hand

That chillness comforts me

She floor me a tale

With her choppers

Laughs like a venus

She is my granny

© Sweetlin Anisha R

Zeenat

Sweet smile

There is curve down my nose

Which shows white diamond

Smile kills torment

Smile with your full soul

Smile rubs tears

Smile gives sweet snap

Smile gives positivity

Spread smile with everyone

© Sweetlin Anisha R

To Readers –

Keep smiling, it is the best ointment for your pains.

Keep smiling, when your heart is too heavy and tears won't come.

Keep smiling, when you can't handle any situation and leave it to God.

Keep smiling, when something is happening exactly opposite of what you want because there will be definitely a reason behind it.

Keep a smile on your face and try to cheer up always because before anything you have to heal yourself. You are the only one who truly loves you and with you till your last breath.

That's exactly will be the **Smile Of The Face** that you need to live again.

- Zeenat